To _____

From _____

If Forever Came Tomorrow . . .

These Are The Things I'd Like To Do Today

Lee J. Painter

LONGSTREET PRESS
Atlanta, Georgia

Published by LONGSTREET PRESS, INC.,
a subsidiary of Cox Newspapers,
a division of Cox Enterprises, Inc.
2140 Newmarket Parkway
Suite 118
Marietta, Georgia 30067

Printed in the United States of America

3rd printing, 1994

Library of Congress Catalog Number 93-79665

ISBN: 1-56352-108-3

This book was printed by Semline Incorporated, Westwood, Massachusetts.

Jacket and book design by Jill Dible

If Forever Came Tomorrow . . .

These Are The Things I'd Like To Do Today

*T*ouch the warm
spot where a deer has
spent the night.

*L*isten to the sounds
of a playground.

*S*ee the lights of Paris
at midnight.

*K*now the sound
of Lincoln's voice.

*S*ee my parents as each
one was as a child.

Stretch out under a
giant oak and watch
the pattern of its arms
reach to the sky.

*T*each a child a
song she will still be
happily humming in
fifty years.

Crawl into bed with
a cup of tea, a good
book, and my cats.

Play a symphony on a
blade of grass.

*H*old my father's hand.

*S*ay, I'm sorry.

*G*ive a lame dog the legs
to run free.

Remember that a child's days aren't just preparation for life but that they are life.

Instead of looking for
the quiet corners of the
world, look for the quiet
corners of my heart.

*B*e as graceful and grand as a hawk gliding.

*B*e as truthful as handwriting.

Be less concerned
with where I'm going
than with the wake
I'm leaving.

Give an old man a
red racer and a good
downhill shove.

Hold a sleeping child.

Listen to a distant waterfall through a forest in the fall.

Inhale the smells of an artist's studio, or a carpenter's workshop.

*T*ake back all the
times I scolded and
yelled when I could have
laughed and hugged.

*L*ove my work the way a gardener loves the tender new green of spring.

*S*tand with my friends
and together sing the
words of old hymns.

*I*nhale the sweet, clean
smells of a baby.

Sit by a warm fire with
my grandmother.

Treat pettiness as I would
treat flies or gnats.

*H*ave the energy of a
two-year-old at the park.

*B*e the wind and touch
every twig and chime.

*B*e as welcome as a
daffodil in a February drizzle.

*T*ell my sister that she has
been my good friend.

Give the deaf the
sounds of rainfall,
birdsong, or Bach.

Be a child again, quietly
listening to the unhurried
voices of my family from the
safety of a front porch swing
on a Sunday afternoon.

Smell fresh-cut pine.

Cry like I have not
cried in years.

*C*atch the first scent
of fall in the air.

*L*augh until it hurts.

*S*peak the languages of
people I don't understand.

*H*ave a dinner of
conversation with six
courses of friends.

*K*now what it is like
to stand as a tree.

*T*ell my mother she
did a good job.

Be more concerned that
I'm always learning than
that I'm always teaching.

Remember that life is not
art but that living is.

*L*et a bar of Swiss
chocolate melt on my
tongue.

*H*ear the echoes of
organ music.

· 30 ·

Stand under a full
October moon.

*B*e a friend to
someone who has
never known one and
never would.

*B*e as full of
possibility as an adored
and respected child.

*W*atch Monet paint.

Watch a young boy race his dog across a wide field.

Drink a cup full of sweetness
from a honeysuckle vine.

Give a 50-year-old man
who has never read the gift
of written words.

*B*e as calm and
peaceful as sea surface
after a storm.

*W*atch a potter at work.

Give the blind the gift
of a rainbow, a sunset, or
a Matisse.

Drive a roadster as fast as I
can on an open country road.

Smell nuts roasting on the busy sidewalks of New York or Rome.

*S*ee the faces of my
ancestors in their prime.

*B*e held by the one
I love.

*S*mell the simple
pleasures of
just-turned soil.

*E*at a warm biscuit
with melted butter and
pear preserves.

*H*ear Christmas carols
sung in the snow.

Ride the currents
of a laugh and the
ripple of an intelligent
thought.

Sit in the branches of
an ancient tree.

Watch colors pour
through the windows of
a quiet church.

Sleep outside through
one full night.

Walk in Shakespeare's
shadow for an hour.

*S*ay to those who should have been told it: You were right and I was wrong.

*F*or just one moment let
the earth take a rest.

*H*ear the summer night
music of katydids.

Stand beside a deafening sea.

· 49 ·

Give back to every child
each moment they were ever
rushed or ridiculed.

Stop blaming others for
the things in my life that
don't get done.

*W*atch a speckled trout
swimming in a clear,
clean stream.

*S*ee the world through
a four-year-old's eyes.

Walk with an old
woman into the night
and let her dance like
a girl on a breeze.

*L*et each child know

what it is to be loved

and wanted and safe.

*L*et each adult know

what it is to be the most

important person in

someone else's life.

Wherever I might
automatically give one,
remind myself to give two.

Not regret the past.

IF FOREVER CAME TOMORROW,

I would live today.

IF FOREVER CAME TOMORROW,

I would be grass, hill, hoof, tree.

I would be bone, feather, stone, sea.

I would be wrinkle, tear, skin, hand.

I would be brain, sight, and memory.

IF FOREVER CAME TOMORROW,

I would see you through the night.

I would speak your name for always and

say what maybe I have not said in years.

I would say, You are good.

You are of great value.

And you are loved.

ILLUSTRATION CREDITS: